# Big Tom
## The Inverted Horse

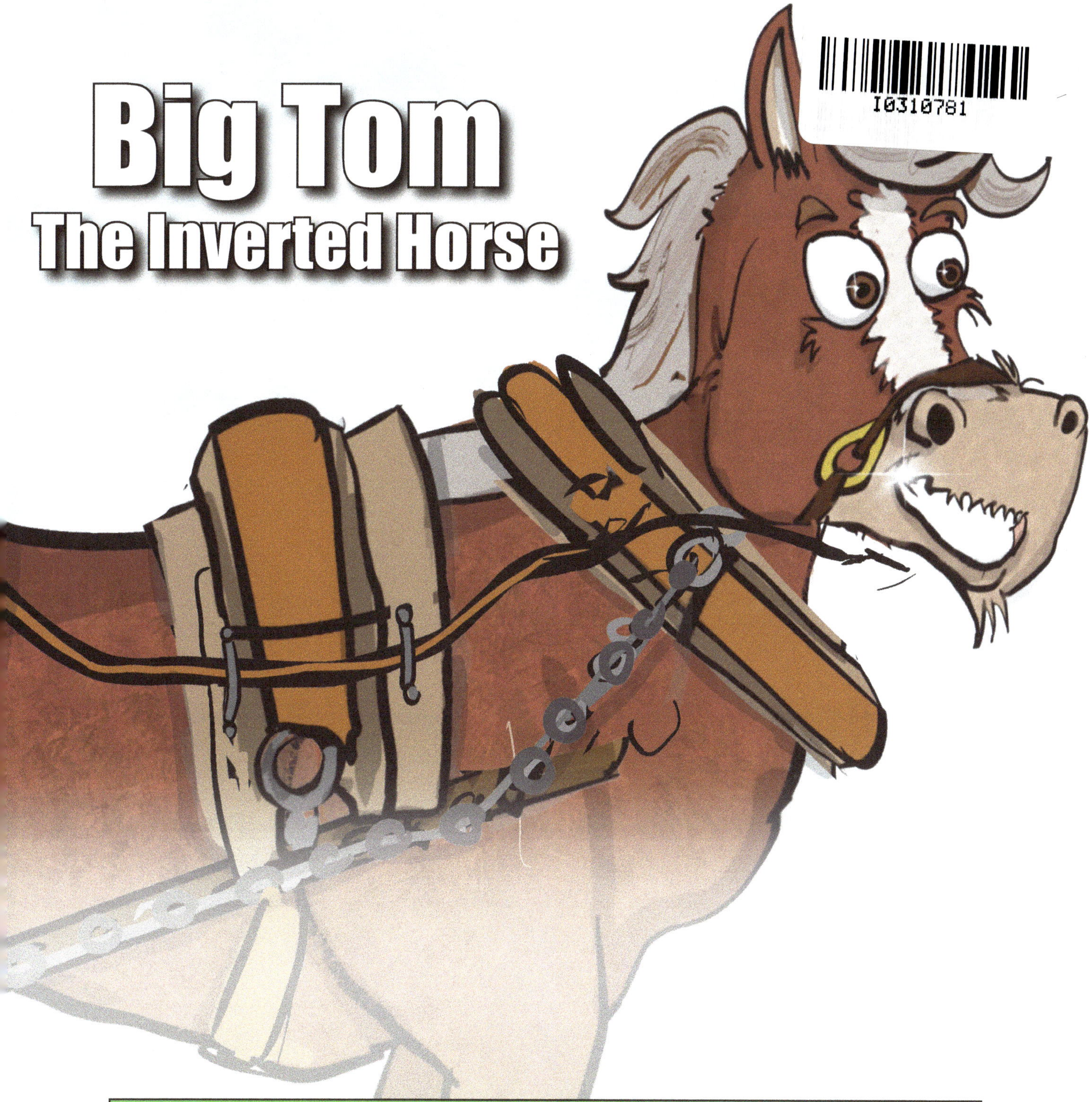

# John Tapley
# Dave Bolt

*An Almost Human Publication*

This is the story of Big Tom the inverted horse.

What's an inverted horse? asked Henri.

If you invert something, you turn it upside down or downside up. It depends on whether you are a glass half-full or a glass half-empty person.

Great Grandad let out a chuckle. An inverted horse can see up his own nose.

All other quadrupeds look down their noses.

Have you ever seen an inverted horse?
Henri shook his head.

Well, let me tell you a story.

A young boy called John lived on a dairy farm in the Big Karri Country of Walpole.

His dad worked at the local timber mill. Money was pretty tight in those days.

John was one of nine children. He had five sisters and three brothers. One day, a big Karri tree fell on one of the fences and John had to fix it.

He was the only one who knew what to do. His dad was at work all day and he was the eldest boy.

He got the trusty, old Clydesdale horse

# Big Tom

Big Tom was harnessed to the cart. The dragsaw was hitched behind and off they went.

John cut the tree into three pieces with the mighty dragsaw. Then using a chain hooked to the cart's axle, Big Tom pulled the timber away from the fence.

The fence was fixed.

Big Tom rolled two of the logs away so they could be burned later.

There was one more big log left, with a heave John hooked a chain onto a forked branch. This was the wrong thing to do. He should have hooked it onto the stem.

Things went okay for a while, but then the forked branch got caught on the other logs.

This stopped the good steed, indeed!

Big Tom wasn't a quitter. He pulled and he pulled and he...

The Strong Horse was straining and things started to get rough.

He was...

John hit the ground on his hands and knees. He had to quickly scramble over the logs before the cart came crashing down.

John's eyes grew wide. Oops! Now he had an inverted horse. Big Tom's hooves flew around wildly like winds socks in a thunderstorm.

John managed to unhook Big Tom and he scrambled to his feet. Amazingly, neither Big Tom or little John were seriously hurt.

What a miracle!

John looked towards the house and thanked God for looking after them.

He was relieved Mum had not seen a thing.

His parents were saved from hearing this story. It was the least he could do for them.

This story gives insight to life in the early farming settlements in south west Western Australia, and the hard working spirit of pioneering people who tackled daily challenges with great determination and resilience. Such qualities are to be admired and celebrated and remembered, and should be taught and modelled to the next generation.

Author John Tapley is born and bred in Western Australia. He is married, has six children, 15 grandchildren and so far, one great-grandchild. His family and friends have grown up hearing countless stories of his joyful escapades. John has definitely lived a lifetime with his cup overflowing. His deep love for the land he grew up on, his family, and the beauty and wonder of creation, is heartfelt and endearing.

Illustrator Dave Bolt loves to make great stories come to life. He also offers schools and groups a chance to explore their creativity and release their inner artists by running cartooning and publishing workshops, mentoring and motivational speaking services.

www.davebolt.com.au

www.ingramcontent.com/pod-product-compliance
Lightning Source LLC
Chambersburg PA
CBHW041712290426
44109CB00028B/2854